CENGAGE Learning

Nonfiction Classics for Students, Volume 2

Staff

Editor: Elizabeth Thomason.

Contributing Editors: Reginald Carlton, Anne Marie Hacht, Michael L. LaBlanc, Ira Mark Milne, Jennifer Smith.

Managing Editor, Literature Content: Dwayne D. Hayes.

Managing Editor, Literature Product: David Galens.

Publisher, Literature Product: Mark Scott.

Content Capture: Joyce Nakamura, *Managing Editor*. Sara Constantakis, *Editor*.

Research: Victoria B. Cariappa, *Research Manager*. Cheryl Warnock, *Research Specialist*. Tamara Nott, Tracie A. Richardson, *Research Associates*. Nicodemus Ford, Sarah Genik, Timothy Lehnerer, Ron Morelli, *Research Assistants*.

Permissions: Maria Franklin, *Permissions Manager*. Shalice Shah-Caldwell, *Permissions Associate*. Jacqueline Jones, *Permissions Assistant*.

Manufacturing: Mary Beth Trimper, *Manager, Composition and Electronic Prepress*. Evi Seoud, *Assistant Manager, Composition Purchasing and Electronic Prepress*. Stacy Melson, *Buyer*.

Imaging and Multimedia Content Team: Barbara Yarrow, *Manager*. Randy Bassett, *Imaging Supervisor*. Robert Duncan, Dan Newell, *Imaging Specialists*. Pamela A. Reed, *Imaging Coordinator*. Leitha Etheridge-Sims, Mary Grimes, David G. Oblender, *Image Catalogers*. Robyn V. Young, *Project Manager*. Dean Dauphinais, *Senior Image Editor*. Kelly A. Quin, *Image Editor*.

Product Design Team: Kenn Zorn, *Product Design Manager*. Pamela A. E. Galbreath, *Senior Art Director*. Michael Logusz, *Graphic Artist*.

agency, institution, publication, service, or individual does not imply endorsement of the editors or publisher. Errors brought to the attention of the publisher and verified to the satisfaction of the publisher will be corrected in future editions.

This publication is a creative work fully protected by all applicable copyright laws, as well as by misappropriation, trade secret, unfair competition, and other applicable laws. The authors and editors of this work have added value to the underlying factual material herein through one or more of the following: unique and original selection, coordination, expression, arrangement, and classification of the information. All rights to this publication will be vigorously defended.

In Cold Blood

Truman Capote 1965

Introduction

In Cold Blood, published in 1965, was first serialized in the *New Yorker* in four installments. It was an instant critical and commercial success, bringing Truman Capote both literary recognition and celebrity status. With its publication, Capote claimed to have invented a new genre, the "nonfiction novel," and critics quickly accepted his classification, his methods, and his purpose as a new combination of journalism and fiction. He wanted to merge the two—enlivening what he saw as stagnant prose conforming to stale, rigid standards—and he wished to experiment with documentary methods. The Clutter murders were the perfect vehicle for this monumental experiment in reportage.

In Cold Blood painstakingly details, in four parts, the Clutter family's character, activities, and community status during the last days before their murder; the planning and machinations of the killers; the investigative dedication of the Kansas Bureau of Investigation (KBI) agents; and the capture, trial, and execution of the murderers. While the book portrays the Clutters sympathetically, it also concentrates the reader's sympathies on Perry Smith, who, abused and abandoned as a child and scorned as an adult, allegedly commits all four murders. In framing the question of nature versus nurture, Capote's tightly documented, evocatively written account of the Clutter killings asks whether a man alone can be held responsible for his action when his environment has relentlessly neglected him.

Author Biography

Capote was born Truman Streckfus Persons—the only child of a failed marriage between a former Miss Alabama and a steamboat owner—on September 30, 1924, in New Orleans, Louisiana. After his parents' divorce, he was sent to Monroeville, Alabama, to be raised by relatives; this is where he would meet his lifelong friend, author Harper Lee, who wrote *To Kill a Mockingbird,* and who would later assist Capote in the research for *In Cold Blood* in Kansas. He later moved to New York with his mother and was adopted by his mother's second husband, Joe Capote.

Capote had no formal education beyond high school, and though he attended some of the best private schools in New York, he was always a poor student—although he was reputed to have a high IQ. His social acclimation was even worse. He always felt different from those around him, more intelligent, sensitive, and more neglected and alone. He was sent to excellent schools, but it was his life experience and innate talent which would serve as the basis for his writing.

When he was only seventeen, Capote found clerical work at the *New Yorker* and began a relationship with the magazine which would endure through the years. It was the *New Yorker* that first published *In Cold Blood* in serial form, leading to immense critical and commercial success when it was finally published in book form.

Capote had a tendency to base fictional characters on his friends, acquaintances, and himself. His character of Holly Golightly from *Breakfast at Tiffany's* has been read as a manifestation of his own journey from a small southern town to the bright lights of New York City. His favorite, but much older, cousin, Sook Faulk, makes an appearance in his short story "A Christmas Memory," and again as Dolly Talbo in *A Grass Harp*.

He was openly homosexual and left much of his estate to his lover, Jack Dunphy, whom he had known since his twenties, when the two traveled to Europe together. Capote's desire for fame and attention was ultimately fulfilled, and he was the darling of New York society as an adult, but the emotional trauma he suffered while researching and writing *In Cold Blood* would be difficult to overcome.

Capote died in Los Angeles, on August 25, 1984, at the age of 59, the victim of alcoholism and drug addiction. At the time of his death, he claimed to be working on a novel, *Answered Prayers*, which was published in its unfinished form in 1986.

The Last to See Them Alive

The first part of *In Cold Blood* establishes the Clutter family and the duo of Hickock and Smith on two different but inevitably intersecting paths. In the small town of Holcomb, Kansas, the Clutter family's activities are ill-fated: Herb Clutter, the father, takes out a forty-thousand-dollar life insurance policy, and the family does not lock the doors to their house. Each member of the family residing in the palatial house at the center of the successful River Valley Farm is painted with delicate, exacting strokes. Kenyon is a boy's boy, not interested in girls yet at fifteen years of age but a talented carpenter and fisherman nonetheless. Nancy is the town sweetheart, helpful, generous, attractive, and accomplished. She is dating Bobby Rupp, the school basketball star, who is also the last to see the family alive. Perhaps the most tragic member is Bonnie Clutter, the mother, who has been afflicted with a nervous disorder that keeps her confined to her room. The Bible next to her bed is marked at the passage which reads, "Take ye heed, watch and pray; for ye knows not when the time is." The Clutters are a pious and devout Methodist family.

At the same time, Perry Smith is meeting Dick Hickock four hundred miles away in Olathe,

Kansas. Hickock had heard about Clutter's prosperity from a former cellmate who had worked on the farm as a hired hand. Ironically, neither knew of Herb Clutter's reputation for never carrying cash, and both believed the house contained a safe, which it did not. The killers' physical deformities are described in detail. Smith is extremely self-conscious of his twisted, undersized legs, the result of a motorcycle accident, which he compensates for by building up his upper body to a grossly disproportionate size. Hickock's face and eyes had been knocked off center in a car accident, leaving him with misaligned and mismatched eyes. The pair purchase the items needed to tie up and silence the Clutters, eat a big meal, and head toward Holcomb.

The section ends with the killers' car arriving at the Clutter home and the discovery of the bodies the next morning. Nancy's friends Susan Kidwell and Nancy Ewalt discover the bodies the next morning, and news spreads quickly. The town is shocked and deeply troubled that such a brutal act could happen in their town, and moreso that it could happen to the Clutters. The owner of Hartman's Café, the local gathering place, declares, "they were as popular as a family can be, and if something like this could happen to *them,* then who's safe, I ask you?" The killings spark an instantaneous and continuous distrust of one another among the townspeople, as most are convinced that the killer is "one of them." By juxtaposing the Clutters' and the killers' activities in this manner and refusing to divulge the sordid details immediately, Capote wrings maximum suspense out of the sequence of events.

Persons Unknown

Four close friends of Herb Clutter arrive at the house to clean up the scene and burn the tainted clothing and furnishings. Eighteen Kansas Bureau of Investigation agents are assigned to the case. The four primary agents are Alvin Dewey, the chief investigator; Harold Nye; Clarence Duntz; and Roy Church. The bodies of the Clutters are prepared for burial, with each corpse's head wrapped in a huge "cocoon" of cotton and sprinkled with a sparkly substance. The two surviving daughters, now the heirs of the Clutter fortune, arrive for the funerals. Beverly Clutter, who had planned to be married at Christmas, moves up the wedding to follow directly after the funeral, out of a sense of thrift, as all the extended relatives are already in town—and, in Capote's opinion, out of a certain callousness.

Agent Dewey and the others are confounded by what seems to be a robbery-homicide that netted less than fifty dollars and a portable radio. Other theories are entertained, but Dewey keeps returning to the idea of strangers committing theft. He is perplexed by the odd manner in which the Clutters were bound; Nancy and her mother were tied but then tucked in their beds. Herb's throat was slashed and he was also bound and gagged, but his body rested on a mattress box, seemingly for comfort. The killers had put a pillow under Kenyon's head before shooting him in the face. A few days later, someone is caught lurking in the Clutter house, but he turns out to be a curious trespasser. The townspeople are growing anxious and want to see justice served, whether or not the agents are ready. "Why don't you arrest somebody?" one of the patrons at Hartman's Café asks Agent Dewey. "That's what you're paid for."

Smith and Hickock leave for Mexico after the killings, as planned, where they meet up with a German tourist, Otto, and his companion, a man referred to as the Cowboy. Otto pays their expenses in Acapulco and draws several sketches of Smith and Hickock, some in the nude. When Smith sorts through mementos, trying to decide what to keep and what to send on to Las Vegas, the reader is given an opportunity to read a letter written by his only surviving sister, Beverly Johnson, whom he detests; notes on the letter written by his prison mate, Willie Jay; and a short biography of Smith written by his father. After his parents separated, Smith lived with an alcoholic mother who became a prostitute; a brother and sister who committed suicide; and a father whose fanciful dreams kept Smith moving from place to place, unable to continue his education past the third grade.

In a series of convent orphanages and reform schools, Smith suffered physical and emotional abuse at the hands of custodians who routinely humiliated him for bedwetting; some who tried to drown him as a means of punishment; and an invariable lack of compassion or stability. Then and even now, as an adult, Smith often dreamed of a giant, yellow bird that would lunge down, attack his tormentors, and rescue him, flying him away to paradise. In his twenties, Smith has a falling out with his father. They had built a hunting lodge in Alaska, a venture which quickly failed, and after a violent episode where each tried to kill the other, they parted ways.

The Answer

On a tip from a former cellmate of Hickock's, Floyd Wells, Smith and Hickock become the prime suspects. Wells had once worked for Herb Clutter as a hired farmhand and is the one who had described Clutter's apparent wealth to Hickock in prison, a description that ultimately led to the Clutter murders. When Wells hears of the Clutter murders on the radio, he informs authorities. Agent Nye receives a tip that Smith and Hickock are back in Kansas, having left Mexico when they ran out of money. Their plan was, in fact, to "pass a lot of hot paper," or bad checks, around Kansas to raise cash, then leave for Florida. The agents visit Hickock's parents and Smith's sister and question them, under the guise of pursuing Smith and Hickock for parole violations and bouncing checks. The agents hear that the killers are in Kansas, but lose them. Through a bulletin alerting law enforcement officials that Smith and Hickock are driving a stolen vehicle with Kansas license plates, the pair are apprehended in Las Vegas, where they had gone after squandering their money in Miami. Agents Dewey, Nye, Duntz, and Church split up to question the two killers separately, and Hickock eventually confesses everything. Smith, disgusted that Hickock broke so easily, confesses as well and confirms most of Hickock's story.

The killers lay out the gruesome details of the murder, from planning to execution. Once the pair had entered the Clutter house and discovered there was no safe and very little cash on hand, they proceeded with the murders, leaving, as Hickock had promised, "no witnesses." Smith reveals that Hickock, who had a penchant for young girls, was about to rape Nancy Clutter, but that he stopped Hickock. As he put it, Smith cannot stand people who are unable to control their sexual impulses and had threatened to fight Hickock if he attempted to rape Nancy. Smith also recalls in his confession the disgust and shame he felt as he groped for a silver dollar which had rolled beneath Nancy's bureau, feeling that he had indeed reached a new low and that he was sick of being enslaved to temporary sources of money.

Smith proceeds downstairs, where he slits Herb Clutter's throat. Dewey, listening to the confessions, feels that the killings are a kind of "psychological accident, virtually an impersonal act," performed in misdirected rage on people who were so representative of success and normality that they were essentially faceless. When Smith and Hickock are extradited to Kansas, the crowd of people awaiting them outside the courthouse has a similar reaction, as if they were "surprised to find them humanly shaped." Holcomb had wanted and needed an extraordinary physiology, or a cruel motive that they could understand. The appearance of Smith and Hickock, and their booty of forty-some-odd dollars and a radio satisfied neither urge.

The Corner

Smith and Hickock are kept in separate cells of the county prison. Smith wants to amend Hickock's confession to state that he, Smith, killed all four Clutters. His reason for this, he claims, is to give Hickock's mother peace of mind. Dewey refuses this request. Smith and Hickock continue their mutual love-hate relationship, wherein each annoys and disgusts the other, but they are tied by this act of murder and their own insecurities. Dr. Jones, a court-appointed psychiatrist, asks the two to write their life histories. Smith's is rambling and detailed, revealing more about his dreadful childhood; Hickock's is succinct and generic. Extensive, detailed psychiatric profiles of both killers, written by Dr. Jones, appear in full text. The two killers are not able to utilize the insanity plea to their benefit, because Kansas applies the M'Naughten Rule in its death penalty cases, which states that if the accused could distinguish right from wrong at the time of the crime, that person is legally sane. The two are ultimately found guilty at trial and given the death penalty.

Smith, desperate for friendship, becomes friendly with Mrs. Meier, the sheriff's wife, who cooks him meals and lures a squirrel, which he names Big Red, into his cell. He also begins a correspondence with Don Cullivan, an Army acquaintance who writes Smith upon hearing about the case. Once Smith and Hickock are transferred to Death Row at Kansas State Penitentiary, also known as "the Corner," they slowly drift apart, as Hickock begins a crusade to get an appeal and Smith goes on a hunger strike. Capote includes descriptions of several other inmates in the Corner, including Lowell Lee Andrews, who had killed his entire family, and two young men, George York and James Latham, who had gone on an unexplainable killing spree in the South. Hickock is successful; a young attorney by the name of Russell Schultz takes on their appeal and puts their case through the legal workings, giving Smith and Hickock almost two thousand more days in the Corner before they are finally executed on April 14, 1965. Capote and Dewey both witness the execution. Hickock gives his injured eyes to medicine, as some sort of twisted joke, and Smith makes a short statement apologizing for his act. Dewey notes that he cannot feel vindicated by Smith's death, because of the overwhelming "aura of an exiled animal" that surrounded the killer in life and during his execution.

In the final scene of the book, Dewey and Susan Kidwell, Nancy Clutter's friend, meet in the cemetery. Dewey learns that Susan has enrolled at the university that she and Nancy had planned to attend together, and that Nancy's former boyfriend is now married. Dewey's own children are about to enter college. With the "whisper of wind-voices in wind-bent wheat" behind him, Dewey leaves the cemetery, content that order has been restored.

Key Figures

Mrs. Hideo Ashida

Mrs. Hideo Ashida is the wife of a Japanese tenant farmer in Holcomb who is on friendly terms with Herb Clutter and his family. She respects Herb Clutter a great deal and makes the fateful statement, "I can't imagine you afraid. No matter what happened, you'd talk your way out of it."

Roy Church

Roy Church is also known as "Curly," due to his baldness. He is the oldest of the four main KBI agents assigned to the Clutter case.

Beverly Clutter

Beverly Clutter is the second eldest of the Clutter children and, with her sister, one of two surviving Clutters. She is away from home at the time of the murders, visiting her fiancé, a biology student whom her father liked a great deal. Beverly is scheduled to be married at Christmas but moves up her wedding to the week after the funeral services for her family members, since her relatives are all in town for the funeral.

Bonnie Clutter

Bonnie Clutter is Herb Clutter's wife, afflicted with a depression, which never lifted after the birth of her last child fifteen years ago. She secludes herself in her bedroom, which she does not share with her husband, and has difficulty functioning normally in even the most mundane situations. Her condition is no secret in the community, and neighbors are kind and understanding, if not sorry for her.

Eveanna Clutter

Eveanna Clutter is the first-born child of Herb and Bonnie Clutter. She is married with an infant son, living in Illinois. She was Nancy's favorite sibling.

Herbert William Clutter

A hardworking, strict, almost reclusive man, Herb Clutter is a successful farmer and iconic member of Holcomb. He represents what many in the small Kansas town aspire to: material success, a good family, and a reputation for straightforward integrity. With a combination of hard work, foresight, and knowledge, he is able to begin and maintain his beautiful, productive River Valley Farm. Clutter is known for not carrying cash. He is a good cook but not a big eater, often starting the morning on an empty stomach. He is a fair and generous employer, a devout Methodist, a public figure who was known as a "joiner." He attended Kansas State University and graduated with a degree in agriculture, after which he married Bonnie Fox, who hailed from a well-to-do family. To the end, Herb Clutter is faithful and dedicated to his wife, although their marriage has long since ceased to be a complete relationship between man and wife. At forty-eight years of age, he is in excellent health. He was a member of the Federal Farm Credit Bureau during the Eisenhower administration, a fact which draws marginal attention to his death outside of Kansas.

Kenyon Clutter

Kenyon Clutter is the youngest of the Clutter children and the only boy. Like his father, he is tall, lanky, and strong, but not athletic or interested in athletics. He is a quiet, pensive boy of fifteen and is a talented carpenter and quintessential outdoorsman. He had completed a hope chest to give to Beverly as a wedding present and was otherwise interested in machines, horses, fishing, and guns. He is "sensitive and reticent," a straight-A student at the local high school, and handicapped only by poor eyesight.

Nancy Clutter

Nancy Clutter is, like her father, an iconic member of the Holcomb community. A straight-A student, accomplished rider, musician, cook, class president, and leader of the local 4-H chapter, she is also known for being generous with her time and friendship. She is dating the school basketball hero, Bobby Rupp, and her diary records typical teenage gushing and doubting about him. Nancy is the perfect all-American girl next door, made more perfect by her small, cliché rebellions: smoking the occasional cigarette or staying out past curfew.

Don Cullivan

Don Cullivan is an Army friend of Perry Smith's who writes to Smith in prison after hearing of the Clutter murders. He later testifies as a character witness at the trial and visits Smith in the Finney County prison.

Alvin Dewey

At forty-seven, Alvin Dewey is only a year younger than Herb Clutter. Dewey is a meticulous, dedicated agent from the Kansas Bureau of Investigation who is in charge of the Clutter case. He is a former sheriff of Finney County, where Holcomb is located, so he is familiar with both the town and the Clutters. He becomes obsessed with solving the crime, growing thin and smoking more as he repeatedly reconsiders several pet theories about the murders. When the crime is finally solved, he feels it is strangely anticlimactic, perhaps because he believed the killings were committed for a more fantastic or understandable reason.

Marie Dewey

The wife of Alvin Dewey, chief investigative agent of the KBI assigned to the Clutter case, Marie is supportive, worried, and disturbed. She has a dream one night in which the late Bonnie Clutter tells her, "There's nothing worse than being murdered."

Clarence Duntz

Clarence Duntz is one of the four main KBI agents assigned to the Clutter case. He is nicknamed "Old Man" Duntz even though he is only forty-eight, the same age as Herbert Clutter at the time of his death.

Arthur Fleming

Perry Smith's defense attorney, Fleming reluctantly takes the case.

Logan Green

Logan Green is the legendary, charismatic attorney who serves as special prosecutor on the Clutter case. His courtroom persona is much admired by both his peers and the community at large. Unlike Duane West, the younger attorney on the case, he is in his seventies.

Mrs. Mabel Helm

The Clutters' housekeeper and the wife of one of their hired hands, Mrs. Helm is also Bonnie Clutter's confidant. After the murders, she goes to work in Hartman's Café, the local hangout.

Dick Hickock

See Richard Eugene Hickock

Richard Eugene Hickock

Dick Hickock has remarkable similarities to his partner in the Clutter murders, although their backgrounds could not be more different. While Perry Smith came from a broken and troubled family, Hickock was raised by two parents in a stable household that was poor but not destitute. Hickock graduated from high school but was denied the opportunity to go to college, and, like Smith, resents the "haves" who experience success. Although he was intelligent, he performed poorly in school and would rely most of his life on his social, not mental, skills. He embodies a peculiar mix of opposites: he is attracted to young girls, but insists repeatedly "I'm a normal"; he is openly homophobic but calls Smith "honey" and "baby"; he is openly racist but partners up with Smith, who heavily favors his mother's Cherokee heritage and is often mistaken for a Mexican; he considers Smith the natural-born killer, but it is Hickock who needlessly swerves toward a stray dog on the road to kill it. Hickock was married twice and divorced twice, the first time at age nineteen. He had three sons with his first wife, Carol, whom he still claims to love. He is the ultimate con man, whose charisma steers much of his course in life.

Mr. Walter Hickock

Mr. Hickock is Dick Hickock's sickly father, who later dies of cancer while Hickock is on Death Row. While being interviewed by Agent Harold Nye about the Clutter murders, he puts most of the blame on Perry Smith, whom he considers a terrible influence on his son.

Mrs. Walter Hickock

Mrs. Hickock, Dick's mother, finds it very difficult to blame her son for his actions or admit that Hickock is capable of such deeds. She even blames the women he divorced or dated, clearing her son of any responsibility for his actions. She later attends the trial and breaks down as the verdict is read.

Media Adaptations

- *In Cold Blood* is the 1967 feature film, written and directed by Richard Brooks and starring two unknowns, Robert Blake and Scott Wilson, as the murderers, with music by Quincy Jones. Capote was heavily involved in the making of this film, and it endures as a faithful retelling of the book.

- *In Cold Blood* is a 1996 TV-miniseries remake of Richard Brooks' film version, directed by Jonathan Kaplan and starring Anthony Edwards and Eric Roberts as Hickock and Smith.

- *Murder in Cold Blood* is a 1998 documentary about the Clutter murders, which includes police photos, interviews with lawmen who worked on the case, and audio from Hickock's confession.

- In 1994, composer Mikel Rouse wrote a musical theater piece entitled *Failing Kansas* with a libretto comprising language from the actual testimony at the trial and transcripts of interviews. Trying to portray intentions of the story through sound, he presented the conflicting voices in counterpoint, in a technique of vocal writing he called "counterpoetry." It debuted at the Kitchen in New York.

Joe James

Joe is a Native-American logger with whom Perry Smith stays while recuperating from a motorcycle accident. James later testifies for Smith as a character witness.

Eveanna Jarchow

See Eveanna Clutter

Beverly Johnson

Beverly Johnson is Perry Smith's only living sibling. She is married, with two children, and lives in a suburban house complete with picket fence and a dog. She seems to have escaped the Smith family's cursed fates. She is afraid of Perry, and when she moves, she keeps her new address a secret from him. She did contact Perry while he was in prison but is unaware that he despises her and wishes she had been in the Clutter house the night of the killings.

Susan Kidwell

Susan Kidwell is Nancy Clutter's best friend. She and Nancy Ewalt, another friend, are the ones who discover the bodies on Sunday morning,

November 15, 1959. As she is the child of a single parent, she and her mother were both quickly accepted and integrated into the Clutter household. After the murders, Susan enrolls in classes at the University of Kansas, where she and Nancy had planned to go together.

Lone Wolf

See Tex John Smith

Josephine Meier

Josie Meier is Sheriff Wendle's wife, charged with taking care of the prisoners' meals and laundry. She is perhaps the most sympathetic person in Perry Smith's life, as she is kind to him, fixes his favorite meals, and becomes a sort of companion.

Harold Nye

Nicknamed "Brother Nye" for his serious, monkish demeanor, Harold Nye is a KBI agent named to the Clutter case. He has the difficult task of interviewing the surviving Clutters and the Hickocks. He is "peppy" and "restless" and works to keep his sharp tongue in check, particularly when his temper gets the best of him.

Reverend James Post

The prison chaplain at the Kansas State Penitentiary is the recipient of Perry Smith's portrait of Jesus. He later testifies as a character witness for Smith, since he believes that someone who painted such a portrait "can't be all bad."

Bobby Rupp

Bobby Rupp is Nancy Clutter's boyfriend, a high school basketball star, and a respectful young man. He is the last to see the Clutters alive, literally, as he spends the evening at their house, leaving only hours before the killers arrive. Although he is initially a suspect, he is quickly cleared of any suspicion. He spends a great deal of time with Nancy's best friend, Susan Kidwell, after the murders, but they are mutual reminders of the tragedy, and their supportive friendship wanes.

Russell Shultz

A young attorney who files appeals on behalf of Smith and Hickock after they land on Death Row, Schultz tries several strategies, but none works. He attempts to float the insanity plea and argues that the defense attorneys' performances were inadequate.

Harrison Smith

Dick Hickock's defense attorney, Smith is reluctant but ethical.

Perry Edward Smith

Perry Smith is literally made of mismatched parts. His atrophied, twisted legs, the result of a 1952 motorcycle accident, incongruously support a bulky, muscular torso and shoulders. He chews aspirin constantly in an effort to manage the pain in his legs and knees, and there are repeated references to "bubbles in his blood" when he is nervous, angry, or apprehensive. Although he has had no formal education past the third grade, he has taught himself to paint, play several musical instruments, including his beloved guitar, and to be a competent grammarian. Other aspects of his makeup seem to be arrested in an infantile state; he has weak kidneys and wets the bed, as he did as a child; he sucks his thumb; he cries out for "Dad" in his sleep; and he prefers root beer to alcohol or coffee. In his youth, his bed-wetting was the cause of much abuse and ridicule at the hands of institutional caretakers.

Smith's personality, like his appearance, is a curious combination of inconsistencies. He is superstitious, nervous, and fatalistic, and his worries are so intense that they almost seem to invite his eventual capture by the KBI. He lies to Hickock about killing a black man in Las Vegas to impress him but is a prude when it comes to dirty jokes. He is dedicated to his father for much of his life, following him around the country as a child and helping him build a hunting lodge as an adult. He joined the Merchant Marines at sixteen and the Army after that, serving in Korea, where he earned a Bronze Star. He has spent most of his life traveling and was uprooted frequently and suddenly by his father, who did not put him back in school after taking Smith from his mother's custody. As a result, Smith keeps hauling around boxes of mementos full of letters, souvenirs, and sketches.

His bi-racial heritage, half-Cherokee and half-Irish, is emphasized throughout the book, perhaps as a reference to the enduring influence of his mother's and father's tragic lives on the course of his. Smith, like his father, is given to fantastic money-making schemes. He feels abandoned, misunderstood, self-conscious, doomed, and enraged.

Tex John Smith

Tex John Smith is Perry Smith's ill-fated father, an ex-rodeo performer who married a fellow rider, a Cherokee woman named Flo Buckskin. After their marriage soured, his wife left him, taking the children to San Francisco. Although he did not contest the custody arrangement, after his son contracted pneumonia, he came for Perry and took him to live in Alaska. He, like his son, had implausible dreams, making his living from odd, but skilled, jobs, prospecting for gold and the like. At one point in Perry's young adulthood, the two build a hunting lodge in Alaska, which they hope will become a hub for both hunters and tourists, but this success never materializes. After a falling out with Perry in which they both threaten the other's life, they separate. He is described by his daughter Beverly as a true man, someone who could cook, hunt, farm, and who could survive the winter alone in Alaska, earning him the nickname of "Lone Wolf."

Alfred Stocklein

Alfred Stocklein is the only resident employee of Herb Clutter's River Valley Farm. He lives a short distance from the house but did not hear anything the night of the murder, due to a strong west wind and a barn in between his residence and that of the Clutters.

Judge Roland H. Tate

Judge Tate is the seemingly prejudiced judge presiding over the Clutter murder trial. At one point, he is accused of having personal ties to the Clutters; he explains that Herb Clutter had once come before him as a litigant, but that they were not intimate friends.

Floyd Wells

Floyd Wells is one of Dick Hickock's cellmates, who had worked several odd jobs in between prison stints, including a period when he worked for Herb Clutter as a farmhand. He gives Hickock the impression that Clutter is an extremely wealthy man who keeps large sums of cash around the house, when in fact Clutter rarely kept cash on his person or at his house. Perry Smith has never met Wells, but Hickock assures Smith that Wells will be too afraid to go to authorities with his connection to Hickock. Floyd Wells does, in fact, tell the authorities what he had told Hickock about the Clutters and later testifies at the trial.

Duane West

Duane West is the young county attorney prosecuting the case. He has as his co-counsel the legendary Logan Green.

Willie Jay

As one of Perry Smith's prison mates from Kansas, Willie Jay is "the only true friend" Smith ever had. Willie Jay, like Smith, is Irish. He is also the chaplain's clerk, and he takes an interest in evangelizing Smith. A farewell letter he writes contains several astute observations of Smith's character. There are hints that Willie Jay may be homosexual, causing Smith to avoid Willie Jay at first, before recognizing his intelligence and uncanny ability to judge character.

Themes

Nature versus Nurture

Capote includes, almost in their entirety, long texts written by Smith's sister, his father, the court-appointed psychiatrist, and his friend Willie Jay, which detail Smith's childhood, motorcycle accident, prejudices, and mental state. The composite image of Smith derived from these accounts is one of an innately intelligent, talented, sensitive being warped and eroded by neglect, abuse, humiliation, and unresolved emotional trauma. Smith's mother, an alcoholic, choked on her own vomit. His brother and sister committed suicide and another sister disowned him. His father moved him from house to house during childhood, preventing Smith from going to school. Nonetheless, Smith has taught himself to play the guitar and harmonica, to paint, and to speak with exacting grammar. He reads constantly and, "being a bit of a prude," avoids vulgar literature and materials. In prison, he paints a portrait of Jesus for the prison chaplain, which leads Reverend Post to believe that Smith cannot be "all that bad." Capote's recounting of Smith's childhood and family life begs the question whether Smith's crimes stem from inherent criminal tendencies, or whether he is pushed onto that path through circumstances beyond his control.

Retribution

The community of Holcomb, Kansas cannot rest until the killers are brought to justice. "Why don't you arrest somebody?" a townsperson asks Agent Dewey. "That's what you get paid for." The subsequent mistrust and insecurity that pervade the town can only be alleviated by the knowledge that someone has been apprehended and punished. Simultaneously, the fact that the killers are outsiders instigates a hope that the killers are "other" than the Holcomb norm. The crowd awaiting Smith and Hickock outside the courthouse is shocked into silence to see that the killers are human, just like them.

Topics for Further Study

- Research the evolution of the insanity plea, from the ancient M'Naughten Rule to the Durham

Test, the Irresistible Impulse Test, and today's Moral Penal Code. What external political and social forces compel the courts and legislatures to amend insanity plea requirements? What cultural shifts or changing priorities or advances in psychiatry required updating insanity plea legislation? What were the landmark cases which established each new step in its evolution?

- Critic Jon Tuttle claims that the influences of Flannery O'Connor on Capote's *In Cold Blood* are too profound to miss. Read Flannery O'Connor's story "A Good Man Is Hard to Find" and compare the characters of Perry Smith and the Misfit. Compare their attitudes toward the families they murder, their methods of murder, their speeches, and their revelations about their pasts. In what way are both the Misfit and Perry Smith archetypal criminals or archetypal psychopaths?

- Some critics assert that the publication of *In Cold Blood* ultimately led to the United States Supreme Court's striking down capital punishment across the nation, a moratorium that lasted into the

1970s for some states. Research death penalty statistics for mentally ill criminals or criminals who attempted to use the insanity plea to exonerate themselves. What are the arguments in favor of institutionalizing the mentally ill? What are the arguments in favor of capital punishment for truly heinous crimes? What are the benefits for society of either option?

- Southern Gothic literature derives some of its grotesque, macabre elements from the gothic writing of the Romantic period, with its horror stories, violent scenes, and gloomy settings. Which components of *In Cold Blood* are particularly gothic? How does this nonfiction novel fit into the Southern Gothic genre? What gothic elements must be altered or subverted in Capote's account of a horrifying but true incident?

Sexuality

Sexuality is at a low but consistent frequency throughout the narrative. Hickock cannot be satisfied by monogamy and is married twice and divorced twice. He gets himself into two engagements while the pair is in Mexico and makes love to one of his fiancées while Smith is in the room. His secret sexual deviance, however, is that he is aroused by young, sometimes prepubescent girls. Smith must keep Hickock from raping Nancy Clutter in the house, and Smith later admits that he cannot stand people "who can't control themselves sexually." There are suggestions that Smith is homosexual, and it may be his need to control and even hide his own sexuality that provokes his scorn for those who indulge in sex casually.

Hickock, openly homophobic, refers to Smith as "baby," "sugar," and "honey," and arrives at the conclusion that he needs to part with Smith, as he is tired of Smith's whining. Smith himself had often attracted the attention of homosexuals in the Army, and had originally been hesitant to approach Willie Jay as a friend because he seemed to be too delicate. Smith thought that Hickock was a good complement to him, since Hickock was "totally masculine." While Hickock is forever proving his heterosexual prowess to Smith, Smith reciprocates by proving his potential for violence to Hickock; this orbit is driven by each man's insecurity about his sexuality.

Fate

Dewey concludes, after hearing the indifference with which Hickock and Smith confess the crime, that the murders were "a psychological accident." Smith seems to have followed a path not of his own making entirely but an unfortunate and fatal series of such accidents, including events after the murders. Capote is careful to describe the sudden and small twists of fate that, in his opinion, bring Smith to the Clutter home: he contracts pneumonia as a child, leading to his reunion with his father, which keeps him out of school from the age of eight; he misses meeting his friend Willie Jay at the Kansas bus station by just a few hours, when meeting Willie Jay would have given him reason to part ways with Hickock; he was essentially forced to return to Kansas after the murders by Hickock's relentless bravado, leading eventually to his capture by the police.

Foreshadowing

Capote points out fatalistic and ominous clues from the Clutters' last days. The Bible next to Bonnie Clutter's bed is marked at the passage, "Take ye heed, watch and pray, for ye know not when the time is." Herb Clutter takes out a forty-thousand-dollar life insurance policy, which pays double indemnity in the case of murder. Well-known for not carrying cash, Herb Clutter also does not keep a safe containing ten thousand dollars in the house, although the killers think he does. The family dog is gun-shy. Even Hickock and Smith's plans seem ill-fated from the start; Smith tears the glove that they plan to use during the robbery, which seems highly unlucky to him.

Symbolism

The symbols in the text serve largely to detail the persona and interior life of Perry Smith. From childhood, Smith has dreams in which a large yellow bird, "taller than Jesus," rescues him from his abusers, pecks out their eyes and kills them, and then, "enfolding him," the bird carries him away to paradise. The figure of the avenging "warrior angel" is both biblically allegorical and reminiscent of maternal and vigilante themes. On the ride from Las Vegas as he is being extradited back to Kansas,

Smith "contemplates … the carcasses of shotgunned coyotes festooning ranch fences." The corpses were hung there to scare away other coyotes, sacrificed to maintain the security of the ranch's livestock, much as Hickock and Smith, while guilty, will be killed and held up as an example to reestablish a sense of security in Holcomb and, it is hoped, to deter other criminals.

The appropriateness of this symbol is further confirmed later in Smith's autobiographical report, in which he characterizes himself in childhood running around "wild and free as a coyote." From his prison window, Smith spies two tomcats scouting the grilles of automobiles parked along the square. The sheriff's wife informs him that the tomcats are prowling for birds and other roadkill stuck to the grilles, which they scavenge as a means of survival. Smith says, "most of my life, I've done what they're doing," and is unable to watch them further. Smith's self-image as a feral creature surviving on the scraps of others' lives is no doubt enraging to him. Smith also develops "bubbles in his blood" whenever he is angry, afraid, or nervous; although the bubbles are probably a physiological phenomenon as well, the symbolic manifestation of rage literally boiling his blood is a powerful one.

Verisimilitude

Capote succeeds in delivering the portraits of small-town camaraderie; a model family; and indifferent, shiftless criminals—with photographic accuracy. He includes an amazing amount of everyday details from what Herb Clutter eats for breakfast to Hickock's drink of choice to Agent Dewey's wife's avocado stuffing. The exact and intricate manner in which Capote chronicles both the people and events of his narrative is a successful example of what George Steiner calls "rigorously documentary material" applied to fiction. The documentary-style realism is enhanced by Capote's often poetic and lyrical language.

Motifs

The repetition of character-specific motifs unites the four sections of the book, providing textual reminders of Smith's and Hickock's natures. Smith's crippled legs, his childhood abuse, his avenging dream-bird, and his boxes of mementos recur at continuous intervals to remind the reader of his misfit status as well as his sentimentality and surprising abilities. Hickock's tattoos, "serpentine eye," heavy drinking, and relentless sexual impulse suggest a morally indifferent and vulgar nature, one that is comfortable breaking or upsetting societal taboos. The dark, open road is a motif associated with Smith and Hickock, symbolizing not only their travels in life but their path to and away from the Clutters and toward their own deaths. The towns along these roads are similar in appearance and offerings, but vastly different from the insular, wholesome, pastoral atmosphere of Holcomb.

Historical Context

National Anxiety

In the 1950s, with the start of the Korean War and Senator McCarthy's purging of Communists from all areas of American life, the possible infiltration by "the other" caused a national panic and hysteria. Julius and Ethel Rosenberg were convicted of espionage and executed in a symbolic gesture of alleviating this anxiety and purging the nation of its intruders and traitors. Unlike Hickock and Smith, the Rosenbergs turned out to be innocent; like them, however, they were killed to restore a sense of order and fulfill a sense of retribution.

Anti-Establishment and Counterculture Movements

In the wake of the Korean War and McCarthyism, concern about the consequences of blind conformity and false American values spawned anti-establishment movements in politics, art, and literature. It was during the 1950s that the Beatnik, or Beat generation, writers published seminal works such as "Howl" by Allen Ginsburg and *On the Road* by Jack Kerouac. Beat signified literal fatigue, a sense of being beaten down, tired, and worn out. In the 1960s, the anti-establishment movements evolved into more severe counterculture movements in everything from changes in popular music to open drug use and the sexual revolution. The assassination of President John F. Kennedy and the United States' entry into the Vietnam conflict fed the anti-government sentiment and disillusionment.

Disruption increased as national borders changed rapidly, American involvement in overseas conflicts increased, and space emerged as the final frontier. The desire to maintain closer, tighter borders within communities, political camps, and racial groups intensified. The increase of communism outside American borders mirrored the perceived increase of different and more vocal religious, gender, racial, and socioeconomic groups, which threatened the status quo. Women and different racial groups protested for equal rights and protection from discrimination, sparking a backlash. Malcolm X was assassinated in 1965, not by a white supremacist but by an African-American who disagreed with him.

New Journalism

New Journalism was developed in the 1960s and 1970s in reaction to the ostensibly objective but sensationalized tabloid news that was becoming the norm. This new style of writing was an attempt to give objective facts greater meaning by incorporating literary elements into journalistic reporting of documented research. To preserve the quality of the times, these writers, according to Belinda Carberry of the Yale Teachers' Institute, wanted to "record and evaluate history by keeping language and attitudes closely attuned and responsive to the style of events." New Journalism did not claim to be a more legitimate or realistic form of reporting; rather, as Carberry says, they acknowledged that "neither objective or interpretive reporting [was] in close touch with reality." Capote joined these new ranks of "interpretive reporters" with his nonfiction novel *In Cold Blood*.

Critical Overview

In 1965, reviewer George Steiner called *In Cold Blood* "more than a book; it is a happening." He cited Capote's "superb journalistic skills" and the resulting text was characterized as "masterful." Steiner reflected the sentiments of most critics, who were impressed by Capote's methods and engrossed by the story, which was written in such a way as to give, as Steiner noted, "psychological order to a piece of implacably authentic, documented life." Frederick Dupee dubbed *In Cold Blood* "the best documentary account of American crime ever written," and in the 1980s, Kenneth Reed, in his book, *Truman Capote*, wrote that *In Cold Blood* was a "virtually unparalleled triumph in creative reporting … supremely orchestrated in its progression and tone." Helen Garson, another complimentary critic, defended the lyrical ending of the book, reminding readers that the story "is not purely documentary" and asserting that the ending seems "completely appropriate to the artistic intent behind the novelistic element."

Compare & Contrast

- **1960s:** The United States Supreme Court strikes down capital punishment laws as unconstitutional; a national moratorium on executions follows. Murder is the most common crime for which criminals are sent to Death Row. At this point, only ten states have no capital punishment laws on the books. From 1930 to 1967, 3,800 people are executed.

Today: States have changed their capital punishment laws to fit the high court's revised constitutional requirements. Twelve states have no capital punishment laws, and far fewer criminals are executed: from 1977 to 1999, a total of 598 people are put to death by the state.

- **1960s:** The use of an insanity plea relies on the successful application of the M'Naughten Rule, which states that the defendant is legally insane if the defendant did not know, at the time of the crime, the nature of the act or that it was wrong.

  Today: The M'Naughten Rule has been replaced by the more complex and psychologically refined Moral Penal Code, which states that, among other tests, the defendant is legally insane if he or she does not have the capacity to differentiate between right and wrong.

- **1960s:** As an outgrowth of new journalism, nonfiction novels begin to become popular. Capote claims to have invented this new literary genre with *In Cold Blood,* which documents and dramatizes a crime.

Today: One of the most popular and established genres, the true crime novel is a legitimate category of reportage writing.

The book has had its share of detractors as well. Critics who questioned and found illegitimate Capote's investigative and research methods pointed out that he never used any kind of recording device during interviews or even took notes. Capote claimed he had trained himself over the years to absorb a large amount of material aurally and then transcribe it later with astounding accuracy. Indeed, when he began to write *In Cold Blood*, Capote had amassed thousands of pages of notes. Reviewers who criticized elements other than the research methodology complained, as did William Phillips of *Commentary,* of a "contrived shifting of scenes giving off an aura of fictional skill and urbanity." They claimed that the book was trying too hard to be poetic, novelistic, and true to fact, to a seemingly contradictory end. Stanley Kauffman wrote in *The New Republic* that the book was "without the finesse, of which, at his best, [Capote] has been capable, and it is residually shallow." Richard Poirer asserted in his 1999 book *Trying It Out in America: Literary and Other Performances* that with this book, Capote has earned a "minor place in American letters." Although the bulk of critics have been kind to Capote and to *In Cold Blood*, there will be those who, like Phillips, regard the book as merely "high class journalism," not firmly rooted in or accepted by the conventions of either reportage or novels.

Sources

Baughman, Ronald, "Literary Perspectives on Murder," in *ALSA Forum*, Vol. 6, No. 2, 1982.

Carberry, Belinda, *Yale—New Haven Teachers Institute*, http://130.132.143.21/ynhti/curriculum/units/1983/4/ (December 12, 2000).

Conniff, Brian, "'Psychological Accidents': *In Cold Blood* and Ritual Sacrifice," in *Midwest Quarterly*, Vol. 35, No. 1, Autumn 1993.

Dupee, Frederick, Review in *New York Review of Books*, February 3, 1966, p. 3.

Galloway, David, "Real Toads in Real Gardens: Reflections on the Art of Non-Fiction Fiction and the Legacy of Truman Capote," in *The Critical Response to Truman Capote*, edited by Joseph J. Waldmeir and John C. Waldmeir, Greenwood Press, 1999, pp. 143-154.

Garson, Helen S., "Acts of Darkness: *In Cold Blood*," in her *Truman Capote*, Frederick Ungar Publishing Co., Inc., 1980, pp. 141-164.

Hendin, Josephine, "Angries: S-M as a Literary Style," in *Harper's Magazine*, Vol. 248, No. 1485, February 1974, pp. 87-93.

Kauffmann, Stanley, Review in *New Republic*, January 22, 1966, p. 19.

Phillips, William, Review in *Commentary*, May

1966, p. 77.

Poirer, Richard, "In Cold Ink: Truman Capote," in *Trying It Out America: Literary and Other Performances,* Farrar, Strauss and Giroux, 1999, pp. 218-225.

Reed, Kenneth T., "The Shift to Reportage," in *Truman Capote,* G. K. Hall and Co., 1981, pp. 94-118.

Steiner, George, *The Guardian,* http://www.guardiancentury.co.uk/1960-1969/Story/0,6051,106441,00.html (December 12, 2000).

Trilling, Diana, "Capote's Crime and Punishment," in *The Critical Response to Truman Capote,* edited by Joseph J. Waldmeir and John C. Waldmeir, Greenwood Press, 1999, pp. 121-127.

Weber, Myles, "Other Voices: A Life in Gossip," in *Southern Review,* Vol. 34, No. 4, December 1998, pp. 816-817.

Further Reading

Capote, Truman, *A Capote Reader*, Random House, 1987.

> Capote provides an introduction to his writing, short stories, nonfiction articles, and excerpts from novels, excluding *In Cold Blood*.

Plimpton, George, *Truman Capote: In Which Various Friends, Enemies, Acquaintances, and Detractors Recall His Turbulent Career*, Doubleday, 1997.

> In this flashy, gossipy biography culled from interviews, Plimpton, a high-society member of the literati himself, chronicles Capote from his early days as a new writer through the glory days following *In Cold Blood* to his last years as an exaggerated version of the figure he was.

Rudisill, Marie, *Truman Capote: The Story of His Bizarre and Exotic Boyhood by an Aunt Who Helped Raise Him*, Morrow, 1983.

> Capote was sent to live with this branch of his mother's family, in Alabama, when he was a child. Here he met his significantly older cousin, Sook, who would become his

favorite caretaker.

Waldmeir, Joseph J., and John C. Waldmeir, eds., *The Critical Response to Truman Capote,* Greenwood Press, 1999.

> This collection of literary criticism on the body of Capote's work amasses articles from periodicals from the 1950s through the 1990s.

Lightning Source UK Ltd.
Milton Keynes UK
UKOW06f1902270817
308073UK00008B/123/P